I0813959

My True Love Gave to Me

A Catechism for the Twelve Days of Christmas

written by
Katie Warner

illustrated by
Elizabeth Zelasko

This one is for you, my dear readers. What a humbling blessing it has been over these years to have my books find a space on your shelves and in your hearts.

I am always praying for you as you grow in knowledge and love of the Faith and shine Christ's light into our world!

—Katie Warner

I dedicate this book to all the Catholic parents catechizing their children in the Faith with truth and beauty. You are the beacons of hope that we need.

A special thanks to my three children: Philomena, John, and Evangeline. God has blessed each of you with skilled eyes and discerning hearts. You were each a huge part of every page of this book, and your advice was invaluable. Stay close to God and His Church, and you will find your whole life surrounded by Beauty.

—Elizabeth Zelasko

Illustrations by Elizabeth Zelasko.
Cover and interior design by Meg Whalen.

ISBN: 978-1-5051-3132-1
Kindle ISBN: 978-1-5051-3133-8
ePUB ISBN: 978-1-5051-3134-5

Published in the United States by
TAN Books · PO Box 269 · Gastonia, NC · 28053
www.TANBooks.com
Printed in India

ALMOST THREE CENTURIES AGO, there was fierce persecution of Catholics in Ireland and England. Some called it a legend, others a rumor, that during this time, Catholics used the tune of the old French song, "The Twelve Days of Christmas," to communicate a sort of catechetical "code" to teach children the tenets of the faith in secret.

It is interesting to note that, in the 1960s, Byzantine priest Father Harold Stockert (1936–2014), discovered evidence suggesting that "The Twelve Days of Christmas" was indeed a 17th-century Irish-Jesuit code, not just an 18th-century English nursery rhyme, as many assumed. While researching at Georgetown University's Riggs Library, he found letters from a Dublin Jesuit to a Jesuit in Douai, France, detailing the song's hidden meanings. Though he documented their contents, the original letters have since remained lost, despite efforts to rediscover them at the Georgetown Library. It wasn't until the 1980s that Father Stockert's discovery made its way onto the early internet, where the hidden meanings behind the lyrics were shared more broadly.

My True Love Gave to Me presents the mysterious code to children (and adults!), unveiling the Christian meaning and symbols behind the popular tune carolers around the world have come to know and love. Christians have long sought to use or "baptize" legends, secular songs, and traditions to bring the gospel into the corners of every aspect of life. This book is meant to help convey the gifts of the faith, and on each page, you will find enchanting artistic depictions of these numeric symbols. *My True Love Gave to Me* is rich with theologically-imbued illustrations, as Elizabeth Zelasko pays homage to various forms of sacred art, from illuminated manuscripts to iconography, from stained glass to classical paintings. I know you will love her pieces as much I do, especially if you reference her illustrator's notes in the back to explore each page of artwork in greater depth.

It is our hope that adults and children alike will enjoy learning more about these number-symbols during the majestic season of Christmas, a season in which the Church celebrates God—our True Love—lavishing His love upon His creation, first and foremost through the gift of His Son, Jesus Christ. His gifts do not cease pouring out, now through the Church founded by Christ, on which is bestowed a mission to carry His love and gifts to the ends of the earth.

On the FIRST day of Christmas,
My True Love gave to me
My Savior who died on Calvary.

O
INRI
W
N
IC XC
NI KA

On the SECOND day of Christmas,
My True Love gave to me
Two testaments
And my Savior who died on Calvary.

NEW
TESTAMENT
OLD
TESTAMENT

On the **THIRD** day of Christmas,
My True Love gave to me
Three gifted virtues,
Two testaments,
And my Savior who died on Calvary.

Hope
Faith
Charity

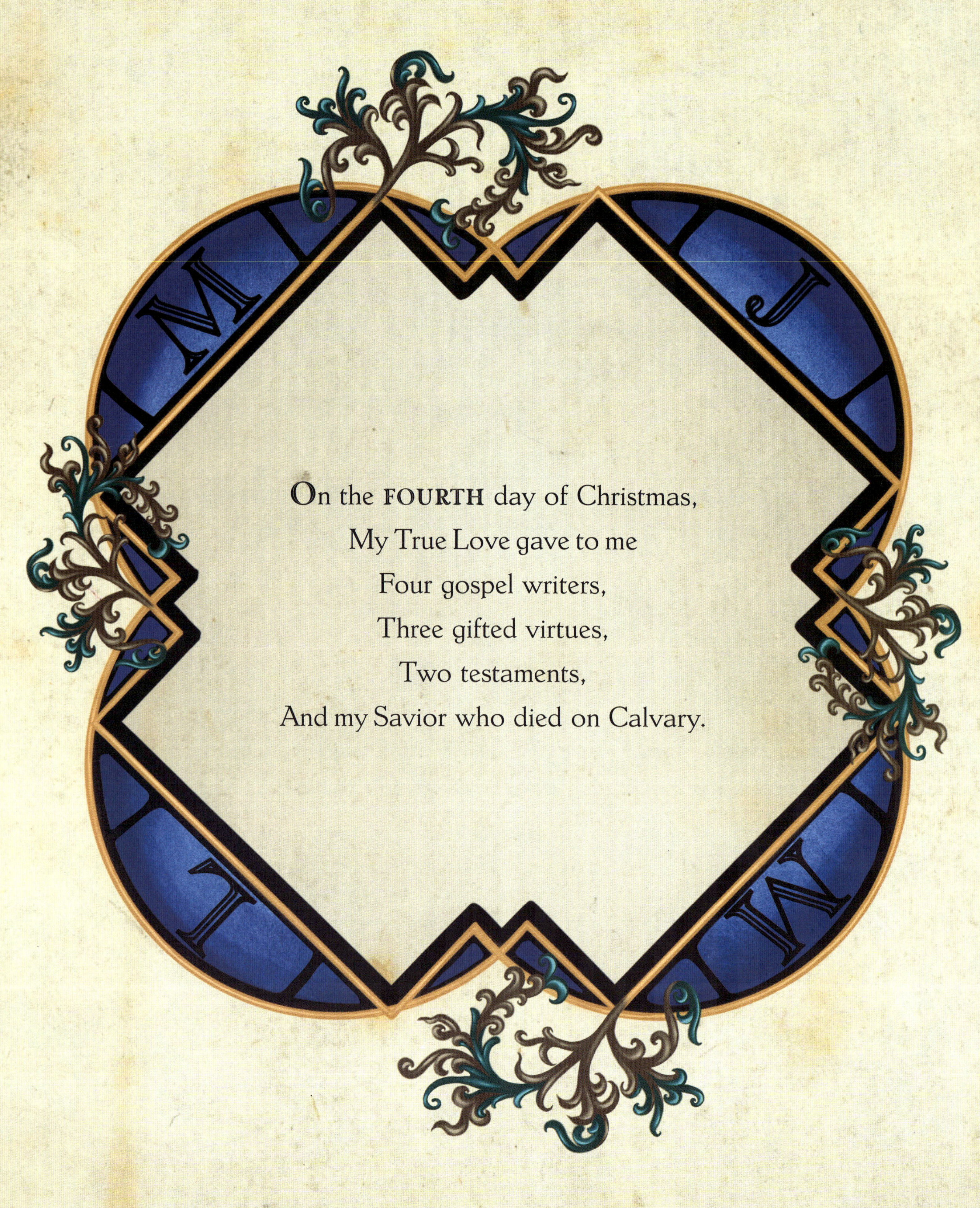

On the **FOURTH** day of Christmas,
My True Love gave to me
Four gospel writers,
Three gifted virtues,
Two testaments,
And my Savior who died on Calvary.

St. Mark
St. John
St. Luke

תורה

On the **FIFTH** day of Christmas,
My True Love gave to me
Five Torah scrolls,
Four gospel writers,
Three gifted virtues,
Two testaments,
And my Savior who died on Calvary.

THE TORAH
GENESIS ∙∻∙ BERESHEET
EXODUS ∙∻∙ SHEMOT
LEVITICUS ∙∻∙ VAYIKRA
NUMBERS ∙∻∙ BEMIDBAR
DEUTERONOMY ∙∻∙ DEVARIM

On the **SIXTH** day of Christmas,
My True Love gave to me
Six days' creation,
Five Torah scrolls,
Four gospel writers,
Three gifted virtues,
Two testaments,
And my Savior who died on Calvary.

Ω
A

On the **SEVENTH** day of Christmas,
My True Love gave to me
Seven sacraments,
Six days' creation,
Five Torah scrolls,
Four gospel writers,
Three gifted virtues,
Two testaments,
And my Savior who died on Calvary.

BAPTISM
CONFIRMATION
HOLY EUCHARIST
PENANCE
UNCTION
HOLY ORDERS
MATRIMONY
IC XC

On the **EIGHTH** day of Christmas,
My True Love gave to me
Eight promised blessings,
Seven sacraments,
Six days' creation,
Five Torah scrolls,
Four gospel writers,
Three gifted virtues,
Two testaments,
And my Savior who died on Calvary.

BLESSED ARE
THE POOR IN SPIRIT,
THE MEEK,
THEY WHO MOURN,
THEY THAT HUNGER AND THIRST AFTER JUSTICE,
THE MERCIFUL,
THE CLEAN OF HEART,
THE PEACEMAKERS,
THEY THAT SUFFER PERSECUTION
FOR JUSTICE'S SAKE.

On the **NINTH** day of Christmas,
My True Love gave to me
Nine fruits of Spirit,*
Eight promised blessings,
Seven sacraments,
Six days' creation,
Five Torah scrolls,
Four gospel writers,
Three gifted virtues,
Two testaments,
And my Savior who died on Calvary.

LOVE
JOY
PEACE
PATIENCE
KINDNESS
GOODNESS
FAITHFULNESS
GENTLENESS
SELF-CONTROL

On the **TENTH** day of Christmas,
My True Love gave to me
Ten stone Commandments,
Nine fruits of Spirit,
Eight promised blessings,
Seven sacraments,
Six days' creation,
Five Torah scrolls,
Four gospel writers,
Three gifted virtues,
Two testaments,
And my Savior who died on Calvary.

אנכי ה׳
לא יהיה
לא תשא
זכור את
כבד את
לא תרצח
לא תנאף
לא תגנב
לא תענה
לא תחמד

On the **ELEVENTH** day of Christmas,
My True Love gave to me
Eleven true apostles,
Ten stone Commandments,
Nine fruits of Spirit,
Eight promised blessings,
Seven sacraments,
Six days' creation,
Five Torah scrolls,
Four gospel writers,
Three gifted virtues,
Two testaments,
And my Savior who died on Calvary.

On the TWELFTH day of Christmas,
My True Love gave to me
Twelve creedal doctrines,
Eleven true apostles,
Ten stone Commandments,
Nine fruits of Spirit,
Eight promised blessings,
Seven sacraments,
Six days' creation,
Five Torah scrolls,
Four gospel writers,
Three gifted virtues,
Two testaments,
And my Savior who died on Calvary.

St. Louis & Zelie
St. Rita of Cascia
St. Martin de Porres
St. Francis of Assisi
St. Joseph
St. Elizabeth
St. Philomena
St. John the Baptist
St. Padre Pio
St. Patrick
St. Anthony
St. John Vianney
St. Athanasius
St. Therese
St. Maximilian
St. Clare of Assisi
St. John Paul II
St. Maria Goretti
St. Mary of Egypt
St. John Bosco

AUTHOR'S AFTERWORD
by Katie Warner

What a beautiful journey! Obviously, God didn't bestow these magnificent gifts upon His creation over the course of a Christmas season or twelve consecutive days, but as mentioned previously, this book allows us to enjoy and explore the intersection of catechetical concepts, numbers, and Christmastime.

Here is a list of the numeric teachings specifically mentioned in *My True Love Gave to Me*:

✣ONE✣

Jesus Christ, Savior of the World

✣TWO✣

Old & New Testaments

✣THREE✣

Theological Virtues of Faith, Hope, and Love

✣FOUR✣

Gospel Writers: Matthew, Mark, Luke, and John

✣FIVE✣

Torah Scrolls, also known as the Pentateuch, the Torah, or the Books of Moses: Genesis, Exodus, Leviticus, Numbers, and Deuteronomy

SIX

Days of Creation, in which God made the day and the night; the sky; the land, plants, and seas; the sun, moon, and stars; the sea creatures and birds; the land animals and man

SEVEN

Sacraments: Baptism, Confirmation, Holy Eucharist, Penance, Unction (Anointing of the Sick), Holy Orders, Matrimony

EIGHT

Beatitudes: "Blessed are the poor in spirit, for theirs is the kingdom of heaven. Blessed are those who mourn, for they shall be comforted. Blessed are the meek, for they shall inherit the earth. Blessed are those who hunger and thirst for righteousness, for they shall be satisfied. Blessed are the merciful, for they shall obtain mercy. Blessed are the pure in heart, for they shall see God. Blessed are the peacemakers, for they shall be called sons of God. Blessed are those who are persecuted for righteousness' sake, for theirs is the kingdom of heaven" (Matthew 5: 3-10).

NINE*

Fruits of the Spirit: Galatians 5:22 lists nine of them: Love, Joy, Peace, Patience, Kindness, Goodness, Faithfulness, Gentleness, and Self-control.

The *Catechism of the Catholic Church* cites three additional fruits (Generosity, Modesty, and Chastity) based on the Latin Vulgate translation, which brings the list of fruits to twelve: Love, Joy, Peace, Patience, Kindness, Goodness, Faithfulness, Gentleness, Self-control, Generosity, Modesty, and Chastity.

✣TEN✣

Commandments:

1. I am the Lord thy God, thou shalt have no other gods before me.
2. Thou shalt not take the name of the Lord thy God in vain.
3. Keep the Sabbath holy.
4. Honor thy father and thy mother.
5. Thou shalt not kill.
6. Thou shalt not commit adultery.
7. Thou shalt not steal.
8. Thou shalt not bear false witness.
9. Thou shalt not covet they neighbor's wife.
10. Thou shalt not covet thy neighbor's goods.

✣ELEVEN✣

Faithful apostles: Judas is the one apostle who was not true to Jesus, leaving eleven who remained loyal to Christ. The original twelve apostles were Peter, James, John, Andrew, Philip, Bartholomew, Matthew, Thomas, James, Jude Thaddeus, Simon the Zealot, and Judas Iscariot, who betrayed Christ. Judas was eventually replaced by the apostle Matthias (Acts 1:21-26).

✣TWELVE✣

Doctrines of the Creed: (Article 1) I believe in God, the Father Almighty, Creator of heaven and earth. (2) And in Jesus Christ, His only Son, our Lord. (3) Who was conceived by the power of the Holy Spirit and born of the Virgin Mary. (4) He suffered under Pontius Pilate, was crucified, died, and was buried. (5) He descended into hell. (6) He ascended into heaven and is seated at the right hand of God the Father Almighty. (7) He will come again to judge the living and the dead. (8) I believe in the Holy Spirit (9) The holy Catholic Church, the Communion of Saints (10) The forgiveness of sins (11) The resurrection of the body (12) And in life everlasting.

There are all sorts of theological numeric symbols not included in this book, which are exceptional to study and then uncover in the Sacred Scriptures and throughout Church teaching.

Here are some of the additional connections not referenced in the text:

1. The oneness of God

2. Natures of Christ (human and divine)

3. Persons of the Trinity (Father, Son, and Holy Ghost), the Magi's gifts (gold, frankincense, and myrrh), the three days Christ spent in the tomb; this number signifies completion (think of repetitions in Scripture and in the Holy Mass, i.e. *Sanctus, Sanctus, Sanctus*)

4. Major prophets (Isaiah, Jeremiah, Ezekiel, Daniel), the Cardinal virtues (prudence, temperance, fortitude, justice)

5. Sacred wounds of Christ

6. This number symbolizes imperfection; the six days of creation reminds us that God's creative work was ordered toward the seventh day, the day of rest.

7. This number symbolizes perfection. We see this number in the gifts of the Holy Spirit (wisdom, understanding, knowledge, counsel, fortitude, piety and fear of the Lord), the colors of the rainbow reminding of the Noahide Covenant, the deadly sins (pride, envy, wrath, sloth, avarice, gluttony, lust) and opposing—also called "lively" or "heavenly"—virtues (humility, kindness, meekness, diligence, generosity, temperance, chastity), the joys and sorrows of Our Lady (joys: the Annunciation, the Nativity, the Adoration of the Magi, the Resurrection, the Ascension, Pentecost, the Coronation of the Virgin as Queen of Heaven and Earth; sorrows: the Prophecy of Simeon, the Flight into Egypt, the Loss of the Child Jesus in the Temple for three days, Our Lady encountering Christ on the Via Dolorosa, the Crucifixion, the Pieta, the Placing of Christ's body in the tomb), churches in the Book of Revelation (Ephesus, Smyrna, Pergamum, Thyatira, Sardis, Philadelphia, and Laodicea), and seals on the Book of Life in Revelation.

8. New creation/Christ's Resurrection (think of octagonal baptismal fonts!)

9. Choirs of angels (Seraphim, Cherubim, Thrones, Dominions, Powers, Virtues, Principalities, Archangels, and Angels); this number signifies mystery

10. Plagues of Egypt (water turned to blood, frogs, gnats, flies, livestock disease, boils, hail, locusts, darkness for three days, death of the Egyptian firstborn)

12. Apostles (Peter, Andrew, James, John, Philip, Bartholomew, Thomas, Matthew, James, Thaddeus, Simon, and Judas), Tribes of Israel (Issachar, Zebulun, Reuben, Simeon, Gad, Ephraim, Manasseh, Dan, Asher, Naphtali, Judah, and Benjamin)

40. A period of testing or trial (think of Israel wandering 40 years, Jesus's 40 days in the desert, our liturgical season of Lent. . .)

There is a certain sacredness attached to numbers in God's plan of salvation. . . Let us not cease to marvel at His majesty written all over creation, down to the last number!

A NOTE FROM THE ILLUSTRATOR
Elizabeth Zelasko

MY PRAYER FOR YOU

Welcome to the artwork of *My True Love Gave to Me*! I have been praying for you. Truly and honestly. You and your children have been on my heart for the many months that it took to render this work. I pray that the images in this book lead you closer to God and closer to the truths of our Catholic faith. Images are a powerful thing. 90% of our learning as children is visual, so what better way to teach the faith than to use beautiful images? It is my hope that this book does not just come off the shelf at Christmas but that it serves as a teaching aid throughout the year.

THE STYLE OF THE ART

The Catholic Church is a treasure trove of beauty. There are many styles of sacred art, and we should learn from and celebrate them all! From illuminated manuscripts, iconography, mosaics, Classical paintings, Renaissance paintings, stained glass windows, and frescos; the way in which artists have portrayed God and the truths of our faith over the centuries are endless. I have taken a moment in this book to visually mention as many as I could while keeping the overall look cohesive and engaging.

HELPFUL TEACHING TOOLS HIDDEN IN EACH PAGE

The Cover

The cover is a traditional Eastern Catholic icon of the Nativity! Here we see Christ, who was born to die for us, wrapped in the same linen that he will be buried in. The cradle itself is even a type of tomb. We see God in the uncreated light breaking through time and space to be with us. In traditional iconography, the icon shows the temptation of Saint Joseph to not believe in the miraculous birth. In some icons, a little devil is even shown whispering in his ear. But as we know, he did not give in to the temptation of doubt! The Jesse Tree, with seven leaves—a sign of perfection—also makes a debut in the bottom center.

A Savior Who Died on Calvary

This illustration is inspired by the Book of Hours, illuminated manuscripts from the 13th and 14th centuries. People have always loved to own an illustrated book of daily prayers to keep their minds on Christ and to honor the Blessed Virgin. This image uses the lovely blue popular at the time from the *Très Riches Heures du Duc de Berry*, the great work by the Limbourg brothers.

I've incorporated many symbols from traditional iconography. You see Christ on the cross, His heart already pierced and the Precious Blood being collected by an angel. The sun and moon are on either side of their creator. The bones of Adam are said to have been buried under the very place that the "New Adam" would be sacrificed for the salvation of the world. The lettering in white, IC XC is the Greek abbreviation for Jesus Christ, and NIKA is a verb meaning "conquers." The letters INRI are an abbreviation for the Latin words nailed to the cross by Pilate, *Iesus Nazarenus, Rex Iudaeorum,* meaning "Jesus the Nazarene, King of the Jews". Lastly, the OWN is another Greek abbreviation typically seen in the halo of Christ in icons, meaning, "I am the I am."

The Old and the New Testament

Inspired by the Christ in Rogier van der Weyden's Last Judgment Altarpiece, a 15th century Flemish painting, we see the Just Judge seated on a rainbow, the sign of the covenant between God and man, holding both the Old and New Testaments.

The Three Gifted Virtues of Faith, Hope, and Charity

This image is inspired by a detail from Botticelli's famous 15th century painting *Primavera*, which depicts the three *Gratiae*, or Graces, of Roman mythology. These women are the incarnations of *Grace*, *Beauty*, and *Charm*. They also represent acts of charity through gift-giving, generosity, and reciprocity. This theme goes even farther back in art history, to the three *Charities* of Greek mythology! When asked to depict Faith, Hope, and Charity, these themes and Botticelli's image came to mind straight away.

On the left: Thinking on a life lived in faith, hope, and charity inspires images of springtime, renewal, and hope.

The Four Gospel Writers

In the style of stained glass, each Gospel writer is portrayed in their traditional symbol. St. Mark presents as a winged lion; St. John as a soaring eagle; St. Luke as a winged ox; and St. Matthew as the divine winged man. This imagery is taken from the Book of Revelation, where John records what he has seen in a vision of God's heavenly throne:

> *"In the center, around the throne, were four living creatures, and they were covered with eyes, in front and in back. The first living creature was like a lion, the second was like an ox, the third had a face like a man, the fourth was like a flying eagle. Each of the four living creatures had six wings and was covered with eyes all around, even under its wings. Day and night they never stop saying: 'Holy, holy, holy is the Lord God Almighty, who was, and is, and is to come."* –Revelations 4:6–8

These four creatures are also said to represent the four corners of the world, with the Word of God reaching out and spreading to the ends of the earth. You can find this imagery in any Catholic church in the world and throughout art history in the western world.

The Five Books of the Torah

On the right: In Judaism, they keep the holy text of the Torah in the traditional scroll form, as shown here. Also shown is how to pronounce each word in Hebrew!

On the left: I have shown how each word is written in Hebrew. Each word is colored to match the corresponding word of the Torah on the right so you know which is which. Hebrew is read from right to left, so you will see this reflected in the list order. God the Father's hand is reaching down, giving each word to us.

The Six Days of Creation

On the right: Taken from traditional icons showing God the Father creating the cosmos. The A and Ω are the Greek letters Alpha and Omega, which are the first and last letters of the alphabet. He is the beginning and the end.

On the left: You will see each day of creation depicted! The Adam and Eve are from Michaelangelo's Sistine Chapel ceiling.

The Seven Sacraments

Each circle in the stained glass design depicts a Sacrament. The censor on the bottom represents our prayers, but is not a sacrament.

The Eight Promised Blessings

I love Carl Bloch's painting of The Sermon on the Mount (1877.) It is the first image that came to mind when I thought of the Eight Blessings. Jesus is teaching and listening, strong yet approachable. While redrawing Carl's Jesus, I added the Sea of Galilee and included local vegetation.

The Nine Fruits of the Spirit

When asked what these are, I will now be able to recall without hesitation thanks to this image! I hope it has the same effect for you. This image was inspired by the great stained glass window at the Vatican. The Holy Spirit is very much alive and pouring out His gifts to us. I hope you can feel that in this image.

The Ten Commandments

On the right: You can see the commandants written out in Hebrew—such a lovely thing to see!

On the left: You can see Moses taking off his shoes in front of the burning bush, and then the hands of the Father giving the tablets.

The Eleven True Apostles

Inspired by traditional iconography, we see the scene of the Last Supper with the Seder Meal laid out. In the dish to the left is the shank bone (zeroa), egg (beitzah), bitter herbs (maror), vegetable (karpas), and a sweet paste called haroset. There is also a bean soup on the table. I have more clearly illustrated the new paschal meal, the Holy Eucharist, that Jesus instituted that holy evening in the form of bread and wine. If you look closely, you will see Judas with his money bag in the shadows.

The Twelve Creedal Doctrines

On the right: It is hard to summarize everything we believe into one image without crowding! Of course, this isn't everything, but it covers a good deal! If you say the Apostles Creed with your children while looking at this image, I think it will be fun to point out many things. We see the Holy Trinity, the earth beneath their feet and the heavens above, the names of saints written in their book, the Gospel writers on all four corners surrounding them, the gates of hell broken beneath them with demons being knocked down and two angels wrestling Death to the ground. You have a scene from the Annunciation, with Mary being greeted by the angel Gabriel. All of these are framed between the pillars of the Faith.

On the left: You will be able to point out different crosses from around the world—our one faith is universal! On the top is the Papal Cross; to the left is the Franciscan Cross, and on the right is the Jerusalem cross. On the bottom left is the Greek Chi Rho cross, and on the bottom right is a Celtic Cross. There are so many wonderful crosses from all around the world! This would be a great time to research them with your children!

"Wake up, O human being! For it was for you that God was made man. Rise up and realize it was all for you. Eternal death would have awaited you had He not been born in time. Never would you be freed from your sinful flesh had He not taken to Himself the likeness of sinful flesh. Everlasting would be your misery had He not performed this act of mercy. You would not have come to life again had He not come to die your death. You would have perished had He not come."

SAINT AUGUSTINE

ABOUT THE AUTHOR

KATIE WARNER is a Catholic homeschooling mom and a bestselling children's book author. Her popular titles include *Oremus: Latin Prayers for Young Catholics* and *One Holy Marriage: The Story of Saints Louis and Zelie Martin*. She has a graduate degree in Catholic Theology and lives in Georgia with her husband and fellow book-loving children. Check out her entire children's book collection at FirstFaithTreasury.com, and connect with Katie online (she loves to hear from readers!) at KatieWarner.com or @katiewarnercatholic.

ABOUT THE ILLUSTRATOR

ELIZABETH ZELASKO studied fine art at The School of Visual Arts in Manhattan before attending Prosopon School of Iconology where she studied traditional Russian Orthodox iconography. She moved to Denver to finish her Bachelor of Fine Arts degree at Rocky Mountain College of Art and Design, graduating valedictorian of her class.

Elizabeth works full time with publishers, institutions, museums, and private collectors, creating commissioned pieces of art. She gives talks on the importance of holy images in our lives, as well as the theological aspects and material processes of writing a traditional icon and how it pertains to our spiritual life.

TAN BOOKS OFFERS SPECIAL THANKS TO

FR. HAROLD STOCKERT and REBECCA EVEN.

Rebecca interviewed Father Stockert as he gave first hand testimony about finding the coded letters mentioned in the introduction. You can find this interview at **www.LiveThe12Days.com**. Rebecca has also developed an online challenge to help families keep Christ in Christmas while supporting Holy Family Hospital in Bethlehem, a primary work of the Order of Malta. Beyond this contribution, Father Stockert was known for his devotion to preserving and promoting Christian traditions. His work continues to inspire those seeking to reclaim the deeper spiritual significance of Christmas, reinforcing the connection between faith, history, and sacred music.

Learning about this 17th-century Irish Catholic Jesuit history forever transformed how the Even family celebrates Christmas. They began by fully observing Advent, then celebrated all twelve days of Christmas, culminating in joyful Twelfth Night Epiphany celebrations. Today, they "Live the 12 Days! For Bethlehem's Sake."

Together, we invite you to help restore the true Christian culture of Christmas—and support the life-saving mission of Holy Family Hospital in Bethlehem, a primary work of the Order of Malta. A portion of the proceeds from this book will be donated to benefit the hospital and its mothers and babies.

Let us reclaim Christmas—one heart, one home, one holy day at a time.

Visit **www.LiveThe12Days.com** to watch Father Stockert's interview, take the challenge, and access free resources to make this your best Christmas ever.

Live the 12 Days—for Bethlehem's sake!

HowToKeepChristInChristmas.com

Find these and other titles from Katie Warner at
www.FirstFaithTreasury.com.

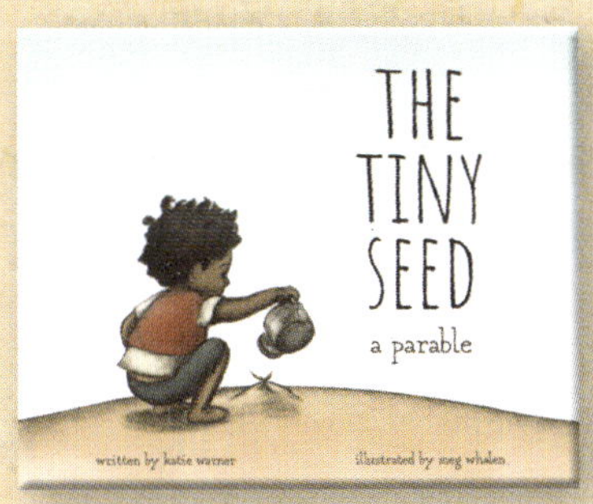